Marshall, J.D.

Please renew/return this item by the last date shown.

So that your telephone call is charged at local rate, please call the numbers as set out below:

	From Area codes 01923 or 0208:	From the rest of Herts:
Renewals:	01923 471373	01438 737373
Enquiries:	01923 471333	01438 737333
Minicom:	01923 471599	01438 737599

L32b

Checked
15/9/11

9/12

- 7 MAY 2002

L 33

1 7 MAR 1972

- 1 JUL 1972

12 DEC 1972

The Lake District at Work

Stott Park Bobbin Mill, set amidst the wooded hills of High Furness, still works today. Its raw material, mainly birch, is cut as coppice locally, then stacked to dry before being turned on lathes. Built in 1835, the typically two-storeyed building was powered by a 32ft waterwheel.

The Lake District at Work
Past and Present

J. D. Marshall BSc(Econ), PhD, FRHistS

M. Davies-Shiel BSc

David & Charles : Newton Abbot

Uniform with this book

Industrial History in Pictures : Scotland
Industrial History in Pictures : Bristol

By the same authors

The Industrial Archaeology of the
Lake Counties

ISBN 0 7153 5104 4

Set in ten on eleven point Helvetica
and printed in Great Britain
by W. J. Holman Limited Dawlish
for David & Charles (Publishers) Limited
South Devon House   Newton Abbot   Devon

Contents

Introduction

The English Lake District is not normally associated with industry. Fortunately for posterity, and for our scenic heritage, the industrial activity of the Lake Counties has been carried on in secluded places and tree-shaded corners, or at depths of scores of feet below the slopes of the fells. The quarry faces have remained harsh and ugly, but all else has been touched by the healing fingers of nature. Even railways have been absorbed into the landscape, and canals (few in Lakeland) are now felt to be so much a part of the English rural scene that many bitterly regret their abandonment.

Without those railways and mines and mills, and without the earlier domestic industries such as the manufacture of woollens or the making of iron, this region of England could have maintained few people in the dales. Until quite recent times Cumbrian farming families were often quite unable to live by agriculture alone. In the nineteenth century it was expected that the young members of almost any family in the fell farms would wish to migrate to the towns. It was a sad irony that as local people left, the tourists came in.

It is not only for purely humanitarian reasons that people are important. Those who love and study the Lake District come to value many aspects of its history and traditions, and to recognise that its unparalleled scenery is only part of our heritage. The people of the region have a character of their own, and the history of Lakeland society cannot be understood unless one is prepared to learn something of the occupations that dalesmen followed at a succession of stages. It is well that one should be able to admire the beauty of a hamlet in the fold of a valley; there is time, too, in the leisure of a walk, to consider how it came to be where it is, or to ask why subtly tinted coppice woods clothe a Furness height. Many a modest building, made of the stone of the surrounding fells, turns out to have been used for some industrial purpose, perhaps only a few years ago, perhaps two centuries ago. The hand of the craftsman is everywhere, in walls, in bridges, in some quietly rusting waterwheel. We learn with John Ruskin, himself a Lakeland institution, that it is not industry which is wrong, but the greed and lack of vision with which it is customarily associated. Little wonder that millions of people crave to escape from the towns to seek peace in these hills.

Lakeland itself is ringed by industrial towns. Not all of them are wholly ugly, nor were their builders entirely lacking in vision. They are very much part of the Cumbrian story, and the people who lived in them, who produced coal, iron and steel for the Industrial Revolution, helped to bring about a world which had all the evils implied above, but which eventually provided some of the means for the ordinary man and woman to travel from London or Birmingham to learn about fell-walking and Lakeland weather. As the motorways will henceforward bring tens of thousands more such visitors, we strongly recommend that they relieve the pressure on totally inadequate Lakeland roads by visiting Whitehaven or Maryport or even the sites of the West Cumberland iron mines. This book should help them to plan an interesting excursion, never far from the finest of scenery. Likewise they may wish to explore the lanes of Furness, or to seek former bobbin mills in the lesser-known dales of the Westmorland—Yorkshire border.

The authors and their friends have explored many rarely visited corners of Cumbria to take the photographs in this book. The story starts with primitive iron-making, which was carried on in almost all the dales, but especially near Coniston Water, by the tenants of the regional monasteries between five and seven hundred years ago, and by itinerant iron-workers in more recent times. Few of the iron-making sites can be 'Roman' bloomeries, as the ordnance map claims. Meanwhile, there sprang up by degrees a host of waterpowered industries, using the energy of innumerable Lakeland streams, and making a continually ingenious use of other natural resources to create jobs and to satisfy needs. The local sheep were the basis of a great woollen industry from the Middle Ages to the nineteenth century, and the local coppice woods provided not only the fuel for iron-making but the raw materials for tanneries, bobbins, baskets, hoops and gunpowder. In Tudor times there commenced the large-scale mining of copper in the beautiful vale of Newlands. By the mid-nineteenth century there was almost as much industry in the dales as there was in the coastal areas; but the rapid development of the Victorian iron industry created a new and different world in Furness and West Cumberland, a world partly inhabited by Irish and Cornishmen and Scots and Northumbrians.

(A general map of the Lake District appears on page 109.)

Early Woodland Industries

The bloomery slag shown here, photographed in a Furness meadow, is evidence of the existence of a primitive iron-smelting industry which is known to have operated more than 400 years ago. The slag is fairly rich in iron because of incomplete smelting. This was one of numerous woodland industries of that age.

The keen observer walking in Lakeland woods and rough pasture will sometimes notice platforms, mounds, stone buildings and holes of definite shape. These, which turn out to have regular patterns of location, include former charcoal pitsteads, and the remains of colliers' or charcoal-burners' huts, limekilns, former iron-smelting sites (bloomeries) and potash pits.

Charcoal pitsteads are scattered in their thousands throughout Lakeland. Many are easy enough to see, because they appear as platforms (of roughly 30ft diameter) in sloping ground in the woodlands, where they display rich flora. In cleared woodland areas they are covered by dense bracken, and on grazing land their forms have become rounded. There may be slight remains of pole or sod huts nearby. The charcoal was used primarily in the early iron industry, although it was later used for gunpowder manufacture also, as is explained in the authors' *Industrial Archaeology of the Lake Counties*.

The former presence of bloomeries is indicated by such names on the Ordnance Survey map as Force Forge, Smithy Beck, Cinderhill, Blomery Beck, Furnace Woods and Low Scaw. Most bloomeries are to be found near still or running water, whether fresh or salt, indicating a need for the washing of ore, tools or the human person—*ad lavandum* in monastic documents. The smelting remains take the form of mounds of purplish-black cindery slag with a deeper admixture of clay, gravel or soil. Pieces of charcoal may be found with the slag. The mounds are quite commonly 100ft in diameter and up to 12ft high. Such masses of slag indicate continual smelting over long periods. The sites are extremely difficult to date, because associated remains are rare in these remote situations, although it is possible that Romano-British and Norse settlers, who of course used iron, worked at this industry. It is now fairly clear that most of the sites are late medieval, or were at least operated in the later Middle Ages, and there is documentary evidence that the monastic houses of Conishead, Furness, St Bees and Holm Cultram got iron in this way. After the Dissolution of the Monasteries, the Lakeland population seems to have engaged in smelting on its own account, and by the mid-seventeenth century smelting was being performed in waterpowered bloomsmithies with trip-hammers and powered bellows. These sites should not be disturbed, and it by no means follows that they contain the early saucer-shaped clay hearths at which the 'blooms' or iron lumps were obtained. Some of the slag was moved by later ironmasters wishing to re-use the cinders as flux material.

Potash pits, also found in the same or associated woodlands, should be treated with the same care and respect. They are deep bowl-shaped pits, usually set into hillsides and varying from about 8ft in diameter and 7ft deep to over 15ft in internal diameter and 12ft deep. The better preserved specimens display signs of intense heat on the lower internal wall surfaces, which are burnt cherry-red. They also have narrow frontal tunnels that may extend beyond the centre of the pit, that is, to a distance of about 9ft; it is clear that these were used to gain a strong draught of air. Two licences of *temp* Henry VIII, relative to tenement-holders in High Furness, apparently refer to such pits as *ealinghearths*, producing *elyinge asshes*. It is now becoming clear (as a result of the researches of one of the authors, Davies-Shiel), that the potash was made by burning green bracken with charcoal, for subsequent use with lime and tallow to make soft brown soaps for washing and fulling in the Kendal cloth industry. There are concentrations of these pits in High Furness and Eskdale, where numbers of medieval fulling mills would need their produce.

In the upper illustration, snow throws the characteristic form of a charcoal pitstead 'platform' into relief (see p9), while the half-hidden masonry of a small potash pit (below) would be much less obvious in the deep woodlands.

Here we see two views of a structure at Winster which has been identified as a very fine specimen of a pit (furnace) for potash manufacture. The narrow, tapering draught tunnel at the front is characteristic, and the general shape distinguishes this from any known lime-kilns in Lakeland.

Early Trade

There was a vigorous medieval trade in salt on the Cumberland coast as elsewhere, and place-names like Salter, Saltcotes, Saltom and Salthouse must be taken to indicate the former presence of saltpans on or near the coast. Seawater was, for example, condensed for salt-making purposes at a known site at Saltcotes, Arnside, where Westmorland touches the sea, and the same name occurs at Drigg, Holm Cultram and Ulverston. The picture below shows the most edifying surviving example of a former salt-making establishment in this region. It is to be seen at Crosscanonby, near Maryport, and was owned by the Senhouse family who played such a large part in developing the latter place.

It was worth £40 a year 'without coal' in 1684, and served the Senhouses during the eighteenth century, until it was closed down about 1790 because of competition from the Cheshire salt industry. The plant was conducted as follows. Deep pits were dug on the shore in order to collect seawater at low tide, and wooden pumps then sent the water through leathern pipes into the large kinches or sleech pans of which three are shown here; one plainly visible over the road, one occupied by a beach hut (and 6ft lower than its neighbour), and another one all but hidden under privet bushes and trees on this side of the modern road. Sleech (briny sand) was filtered in these pans, the brine being progressively thickened until it could be ladled into iron pans and boiled over peat fires, or, as the local coalmines developed after about 1650, over coal fires. The poorest grade of salt was used for tanning, a better grade for preserving meat and fish, and the finest salt for table purposes.

A row of saltworkers' cottages, now derelict, is nearest to the camera. The rough mounds on the far left are tips of coal ash and clinker.

Bridges like that illustrated (Devil's Bridge, Horrace, Low Furness) often symbolise the growth of trade between the fifteenth and the eighteenth centuries. Two types of goods were commonly carried in the southern Lake District during that period; iron, iron ore and the products of woodland industry in general, and wool or woollen goods in connection with the Kendal cloth industry. The modern road illustrated above—the old track is shown slightly deviating from it to cross the beck—follows a traditional route used by the early iron trade of Furness, linking the iron ore mines of the Dalton district to the woodland bloomeries of the Crake Valley and Colton areas. In this instance the route is much older than the present bridge, which is of a fairly primitive type encountered elsewhere in the dales.

The mountainous nature of the region caused its traders to rely upon packhorse traffic until well into the eighteenth century, and the animals were used not only to carry iron and peat or coal, but also slate. But much of the trade and industry of Cumbria was to be found on or near the coast, and heavy goods went by sea from one point to another. The lakes, too, carried their share of traffic.

More sophisticated bridges, with substantial parapets, smoothly dressed stones and wider spans, were built between 1660 and 1760, over the broader rivers, Newby Bridge being a good example. These often reflect the further growth of trade in the eighteenth century.

The Woolpack Inn is one of the very old hostelries in the town of Kendal, and its striking archway, designed to accommodate the large waggons which supplanted packhorses in the eighteenth century, gives on to extensive former stores. The rooms, too, are spacious, indicating that this inn was very much a meeting and resting place for the traders and merchants of two centuries ago. As a date on the central spouting indicates, it was probably built into its present form in the early 1780s. However, there was certainly a Woolpack Inn before then, just as there was a Fleece Inn (Highgate), and a Packhorse Inn, formerly on the west side of Stricklandgate.

The reconstruction of the Woolpack Inn, which is on Stricklandgate, coincided roughly with the rebuilding of Kendal as trade itself expanded. By far the heaviest traffic was on the North Road, from Penrith and to or from the direction of Lancaster, but the so-called cross-roads (from Ulverston, Whitehaven or Barnard Castle) carried an increasing traffic, and were turnpiked in whole or part after 1750. That is to say, they were brought under the control of bodies of trustees (the turnpike trusts) and run on a profitmaking basis with the right to charge tolls along appropriate sections.

The steep gradients of the Lake District ensured that the local roads were far from comfortable to drive along, and the road from Kendal to Ambleside was still steep, narrow and dangerous in 1824. Physical conditions of that kind meant that packhorses, like the one on the inn sign, remained in use until comparatively late in the eighteenth century, and in some cases later still.

Spinning galleries, like the one at Yew Tree Farm, High Yewdale, are the most impressive reminders of the Kendal woollen trade to be found in that area. This farm, like the one at nearby High Waterhead (Boon Crag), and another at Tilberthwaite, is owned by the National Trust. The galleries are open, roofed balconies of no very definite pattern; this one, for example, is considerably longer than other surviving specimens, although it somewhat resembles the large open gallery at Town End, Troutbeck, which is also built on to a barn. Some spinning galleries are simple extensions of dwelling houses, or even passages between them.

The usual theory is that womenfolk of a family sat in the gallery to gain the best possible light for spinning purposes, and that the structure itself is likely to date from the seventeenth century. Again, the galleries do not face in the same direction—with a view to catching the maximum winter sun—and one inclines to wonder whether they were used for more vigorous activities than spinning alone, like combing or carding the coarse Herdwick wool, and also for washing and drying it. Spinning might have been carried on in the galleries during the late summer, and it is possibly true that, as Wordsworth remarked, the old yeomanry gained some profit from 'the employment of the women and children, as manufacturers'. But spinningwheels do not occur with great frequency among the possessions left by yeomen and listed by their neighbours; and it is also known that spinners and knitters spent much time round the fireplaces in winter! Perhaps the truth is that not many Lakeland farmhouses had these galleries, and that they were built by the occasional owner who dealt largely in wool, and who sold it ready cleaned and combed for the spinners round about. Some galleries were used for stacking peat.

Textile Manufacture

This picture shows the remaining framework of a 10ft blanket loom which was installed in a loft near the former Hallthwaites Green Woollen Mill, about 3 miles north-east of Millom, Cumberland. This was one of the earliest woollen manufacturing establishments in Lakeland, with several processes carried on under the same roof or on the same site—spinning, weaving, fulling, bleaching and dyeing. It closed in 1935. The main building (now a home for battery hens) was the fulling and finishing mill. Part of an early carding machine from this mill, and the last piecing machine, are at the Science Museum, South Kensington.

'I am on tenterhooks' is a phrase from the depths of English industrial tradition. Cloth, after being woven and fulled, was stretched or tentered on hooks passed through the selvages (Latin, tentus = stretched). The hooks, as shown in this illustration of a remaining frame from Kendal Fell (above), were fixed into tenterframes lined up in parallel rows on the common, or corporation-owned land, providing space for the treatment of hundreds of pieces of cloth. There were two main tentergrounds in Kendal: Goose Holme by the River Kent, and the sides of Kendal Fell overlooking the town; both were probably used from the Middle Ages. Hallthwaites Green Mill (opposite) had its own tenterfield, and the parish of Pennington was probably fairly typical in having its Tenter Close, while Ulverston had tentergrounds at Town Bank and Newland.

In the 1790s the topographical writer John Housman commented on a visit to Kendal in these terms: '. . . the tentergrounds on the side of the mountain, tier above tier, proclaim the industry and manufacture of the inhabitants'. The frames were in position during a large part of the following century, although, of course, modern processes rendered them obsolete, and the Kendal industry concentrated more and more upon the manufacture of trouserings and carpets.

Perhaps few so-called cotton mills have been transformed into workhouses, but this was the fate of the former workshop (above) at Kirkby Stephen, situated to the immediate north-east of the parish church. It was used by hand-powered jenny or mule operators about 150 years ago. The Kent carpet manufactory at Kendal (1822, lower picture) represents an important development of the nineteenth-century woollen trade in that town.

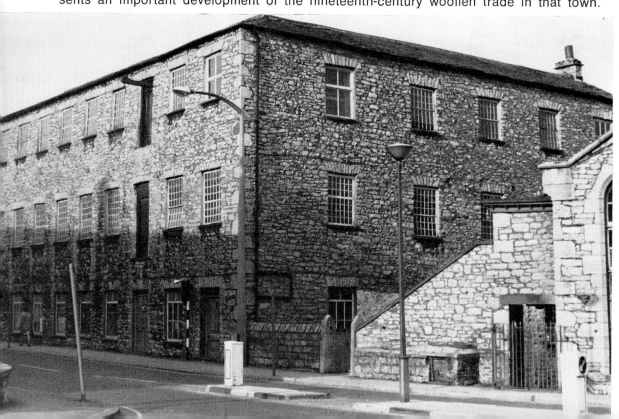

EVOLUTION OF THE TEXTILE INDUSTRIES

Late medieval Lakeland had an extensive woollen trade, although understandably some of the cloth produced was for local use. Clothes were made up in the farmhouse by itinerant tailors, but the excess wool was sold to chapmen or packmen, in the form of hanks of yarn, and taken to be woven and dyed in the towns.

As is well known, spinning was performed by improved machinery or waterpower long before weaving ceased to be a manual process. But carding and fulling, two other important processes, were both waterpowered when the first small spinning mills appeared in Lakeland, and as the industry developed, it remained partly domestic and partly factory-based. In the second half of the eighteenth century, then, the manufacturing pattern was something like this:

1. Wool was produced on the farm, collected by mill or clothiers' agents and washed in soft soaps (prepared, in turn, with the aid of potash pits, see pp 10-11).
2. The wool fibres were aligned or carded for spinning, on water-driven carding engines, usually to be found on the first floor, where picking machinery was also installed.
3. The wool was then spun on manually-worked jennies or, later, by long water-driven mules, on the top floor.
4. The yarn was then sent out of the mill to the domestic narrow-loom weavers, or sent to the ground floor to be made up into blanketing on a massive broad loom.
5. The cloth was then returned to the mill for further washing, and was then dyed and fulled. Fulling was a thickening and felting process, by which heavy leather-padded stocks fell rhythmically into troughs containing fuller's earth or soap, water and the rolled cloth itself. This part of the plant was usually separate, and might have its own waterwheel, as in the case of Rubbybanks mill, Cockermouth.
6. The cloth was then dried and stretched back into shape by hooking it on tenter-frames (see p17).
7. The cloth was next brushed with teazles and the nap raised, and then sheared, dressed or cropped to make different surface finishes. Finishing, warehousing, weighing and packing were done on the ground floor.

Mills of this type also produced yarns for hand-knitted stockings, duffles and 'penistones' for slaves in the West Indies, and the Kendal carpet industry (see opposite) was a direct consequence of the development of the mills. Power looms did not become established in Kendal mills until after the middle of the nineteenth century.

The cottonmills of Lakeland were usually larger structures (see pp 22, 24) and were situated on the main rivers and were also concentrated at or near ports. The flax mills were similar in appearance to the woollen mills, and were also located near the ports, where flax came in from the Baltic or Ireland and where sailcloth thread and cart covers were in demand. These mills weathered the economic climate better than did the local woollen and cotton industries, although Kendal's horse blanket industry was a tenacious one.

This picture shows the top floor of an annexe of the Rawes woollen mill, Staveley, Westmorland, which was rebuilt specifically for that manufacture in 1828. As was common in small country mills of this kind, there were three floors, the top floor being used either for carding machinery or for jenny and mule spinning—more commonly the latter. After having its machinery installed, the Rawes mill was advertised as follows, the advertisement giving some idea of the organisation of the mill *(Westmorland Gazette*, 29 January 1828):

> That newly erected mill at Hugill near Staveley, 33 ft by 49 ft and three storeys high with 16 ft by 5 ft waterwheel, containing 34 ft Lathe frame, 2 Teasers, one coarse, one fine, one scribbler, one double carder, two Billies and one coarse reel on the top floor.
>
> On the middle floor, one fine scribbler, one fine carder and one fine Billy.
>
> On the ground floor, one carding Engine, one Billy, one Reel, two fine-work Reels and one Broad Loom capable of working 7 ft 6 in wide cloths.
>
> An excellent Building nearly adjacent, 25 ft by 39 ft with 3 Storeys with a garret over the same [now removed], and containing two Dwelling Houses, Jenny Rooms, and two Jennies of 60 Spindles each and 4 Jennies of 80 Spindles each.
>
> Also a newly erected Dwelling House with Kitchen, Brew House, Barn, Cowhouse and Stable together with an excellent cottage.

The annexe (of which the upper floor is shown here) is described in the fourth paragraph of the advertisement. When the floor space and windows were measured, the dimensions suggested that the two smaller, 60-spindle jennies were at the far end. The break-line in the floor nearer the camera indicates where the building was extended subsequently to allow the installation of a large mule. These spinning jennies were of course handpowered, but by 1844 this mill had waterpowered mules.

The picture (above) of the Briery woollen mill, Keswick (NGR 286242), is illustrative of a general form and architecture which was common to the nine other woollen mills of this immediate area. These were situated at Millbeck-under-Skiddaw, Applethwaite, Greta hamlet, Fitz, Brigham, Thornthwaite, Stair and Braithwaite, where there were two such mills. Similar establishments, or their shells, are to found throughout the whole of the west and south-west Lakeland. Another important concentration of woollen mills (in the late nineteenth century in that instance) was that to the east of Carlisle and beyond the Northumberland border. The mill illustrated here had a specialised 'line' in fancy waistcoatings in 1829, and produced general woollen goods until after 1894; that is to say, a wide range of processes was carried on under one roof.

Whereas the woollen industry of Lakeland proved to be viable during the nineteenth century, the early cotton factories were overtaken by the steampower revolution in Lancashire, and by the economies of scale and concentration which benefitted mills in the south of that county. Hence it was common for cottonmills to be converted to woollen or other manufacture. This is what happened in the cases of the Birks cottonmill, Sedbergh, (p22, bottom) and of the Barley Bridge mill, Staveley. The former was in existence in 1829, and was spinning cotton in 1848, thereafter turning to the manufacture of bobbins, dyes and woollens at various times. It is now an egg warehouse. The Barley Bridge cottonmill, a very fine specimen of eighteenth-century origin, was referred to several times in correspondence from another cottonmill's owners, for 12 December 1789 (upper picture, p22).

The Birks mill, Sedbergh, (below) is unusually solidly constructed, and has a fine water-course. The Barley Bridge mill, (above) had its own bobbin mill, the building nearest the camera, attached to it in the late eighteenth century; that is, installed as a direct out-growth of the cottonmill.

The somewhat stern facade of the former Ainsworth's flax mill at Cleator (1800 rebuilt or extended in 1859) represents the early Victorian Cumbrian flax industry at its most important (above). This mill was the first flax enterprise to use spools, cops and 3 and 6 cord twist thread for sewing machines. The internal view in the lower picture shows line-shafting supports of the same period, this time at the High Ellers mill, Ulverston, one of the early steampowered cotton enterprises in that town.

This picture shows the largest former cottonmill in the extreme northern counties of England, the sandstone-built Shaddon mill in Denton Holme, Carlisle, 224ft long and 83ft high. Originally owned by the firm of Peter Dixon, it was completed on 25 October 1836, before any railway line reached the Cumberland city. The Dixon firm supplied yarn to many hundreds of weavers also employed by them, working domestically for many miles around Carlisle: the grand total of all employees is said to have reached 8,000 in 1847. Sir William Fairbairn designed the iron framing and roof support system of the interior, which is still used for textile production, albeit for woollen mule-spun yarn, by Messrs Robert Todd & Sons. The 305ft chimney is a famous Carlisle landmark. Built when the mill was erected, it now serves as a ventilation outlet for the Carlisle sewerage system.

THE PAPER INDUSTRY

This view of pulp-crushing rollers at Burneside papermill, near Kendal, may seem to have little to do with the subject of textiles until it is remembered that all early papers made in the district originated in rags from the cotton, flax and woollen industries. Only in 1874 did these particular mills turn to straw, jute, alfalfa, esparto grass, and pulp from Norwegian timber.

These four pairs of Aberdeen granite rollers work on the same grinding principle as that used by limestone incorporating runners in a gunpowder mill, or by the smaller limestone runners in a reddle mill (see p86). Although the machinery is for practical purposes identical, each trade uses its own specific terms. These 'Koller Gangs' (from the German *kolle gang*—a rolling motion) are now being replaced, but were used to crush the raw materials for paper manufacture prior to adding water to make the initial pulp.

Since the pulp was originally of textile material, the earliest small papermills naturally sought to be near a source of rags. An advertisement of 1813 illustrates this siting factor:

Caldbeck Paper Mill to be let . . . A two-vat paper mill, plus barn, byre, dwelling house etc. . . . at a yearly rent of £120, the mill has lately been built upon the most improved construction and with Machinery is in good repair, well finished, very conveniently supplied with water of the best quality from the adjacent river, and very conveniently situated for the collection of rags . . . .

Cotton waste could be obtained from Wigton, and woollen rags from Keswick and Caldbeck itself.

Agriculturally Based Trades and Industries

CORN MILLS

The oldest established and most numerous waterpowered mills of Lakeland were of course cornmills. Many of these were, if in existence previously, rebuilt in the eighteenth century, and the Comb Gill Corn and Saw Mill, Borrowdale, was fairly typical in having been rebuilt in its present site about 1796, replacing another mill further upstream which was washed away by a cloudburst on 13 August 1795.

This mill contained a single pair of Penrith sandstone runners mounted on a plinth against the inner wall at the wheel end. The coarse oatmeal made was shot direct down a stone chute into sacks. On the northern side of the mill is a small square room which was once the drying kiln—an essential part of every Lakeland or other cornmill, since damp corn was liable to clog and to fire the wooden machinery. Fires burning at cellar level produced rising hot air passing through a floor of 1ft-square red clay tiles, each with perforations too small to allow the escape of grain.

Thanks to the work of Mr J. Hughes and the late Mr J. M. Fawkes of Cockermouth, there are now recorded details of some 37 windmills in the Lake Counties, 30 of which were situated on the broad, windy Solway Plain. Most of the regional examples appear to have been built between 1550 and 1800, and were maintained until about 1860. Possibly it was the coming of the railways that closed them. Some appeared at not unlikely sites like Walney Island, Harrathwaite on Kells (Whitehaven) and Broughton-in-Furness, and there are three windmill sites in the Eden Valley, at Lazonby, Hoff and Great Musgrave. This 25ft structure at Cockermouth (above) is depicted in nineteenth-century prints as a mill with four sails, and is remarkable in having been sited so close to such copious sources of waterpower as the rivers Cocker and Derwent. It was converted to a foundry about 1840.

These cornmill runner-stones at Witherslack mill (NGR 448842), which of course are top stones, are about 4ft in diameter. The stone nearest the camera is a French burr, made up of several pieces of a coarse vesicular flint (from certain quarries near Epernon) bound by iron hoops. The action of these stones splits open or 'shells' the grains from the husks, and they are known as shelling or skilling stones. Such stones were already in use in this area by 1821. The wide furrows enabled grain to move rapidly from the 'bosom' to the 'skirt' of the stone.

The more distant stone is a specimen of the best type of flour stone, a Derby grit. It is of simple pattern, with only one 'slave' to every 'master' furrow, indicating that it was used to make coarse oatmeal. In some remote dales, local stones such as Shap granite, slate, Ennerdale granophyre and Penrith sandstone have been made into millstones.

Although the principles of the different types of waterwheel are simple enough to grasp, a closer look at the details of wheel construction shown on this page and the next page will also give some idea of the complexities involved. The water must fall round the perimeter of the wheel through as large a drop or with as great a leverage as possible. The wheel must be of strong construction and long life, and yet be dismantled easily in sections. It may be undershot, overshot, pitchback or of breast-wheel type. The first three terms largely explain themselves. On a breast wheel the water comes in at four o'clock if low breast and at one o'clock if of high breast type.

The wheel partially illustrated here (at Whitbeck, Cumberland, NGR 117846, to the west of Black Combe) is in fact of overshot type. The axle is a solid octagon, with two single-cast flaunches wedged onto it. The bearings and gudgeons are held in by heat-shrunk iron hoops. The bearing is a simple cast-iron box, although anything from stone (as at Boot in Eskdale) to phosphor-bronze (as at Witherslack) was also used for this fitting. The eight arms are bolted into the axle-arm sockets, and sole-plate sockets hold the outer ends of the arms. The buckets or vanes are held between parallel shrouds, and the underside, or sole plate is made of planks or sheet iron and helps to keep the water in the buckets. A normal eight-armed wheel has forty-eight buckets.

Stubsgill cornmill wheel, Cumberland (NGR 019229), shown in the upper picture, is unusual in that it is all metal, the drive to the internal machinery having been supplied through a wheel-ring built on the rim of the shroud. The framings of the vanes can be seen attached to the shrouds, and their shape indicates that the wheel was of an overshot type with a flow of water running down left (anticlockwise) into the buckets—and with the supply, of course, coming from a raised position over the wheel, but shooting forward in this instance.

The toothed ring, as shown in both the upper and the lower pictures opposite, had a very special job to do. The axle and bearings of a wheel not only had to carry the weight of the wheel itself, but were subjected to an even greater strain when the power unit was put to driving a mass of machinery. This twisting strain, or torque, was reduced sharply when the drive was transmitted through a wheel-ring. In the case of the Thwaites cornmill waterwheel (Cumberland, NGR 183867), the original transmission of power to the grinding machinery was directly through the 'bundle of rods' type axle shown in the left lower picture; but when a sawmill was later built on to the east side of the cornmill, the addition of the ring was found to be necessary in order that the wheel could work without undue strain. The drive was passed through the 'ring nut' or pinion shown in the rear.

Not all interesting cornmills are in the deep countryside, and Ulverston's Town Mill (below) carries on a milling tradition which may well date from the year 1234, when the town's cornmills are first mentioned. The Town Mill itself is specifically mentioned in 1678. It stands on the formerly much-used Gillbanks Beck, which served four corn, three cotton one paper and one woollen mill, a small tannery group, a foundry, and at least two breweries, ie through two branches which pass through the town. They are now wholly or partially culverted. The Town Mill was originally powered through an overshot wheel, in the rear of the building seen in this picture; later, a turbine was installed.

MALTING AND BREWING

The long barn-like building (above) by the roadside at Grizebeck, Kirkby-in-Furness, in fact contained a former malt kiln. It served the Bank End cornmill and the Grizebeck cornmill, and was built before 1780; all that now remains of the kiln is the external structure and the massive wooden flooring and roof beams. This example serves as a reminder that malting became a well established industry in areas like Plain Furness, where barley and

wheat were almost as widely grown as oats. The small picture (left) shows a building at Caldbeck, Cumberland, which started its career as a papermill in the 1780s, on the site of a previous cornmill. During the first half of the nineteenth century it became a brewery, and it still retains the louvred windows and roof and the kiln on the left-hand side. This is one of many small breweries which were to be found in Cumbria during the nineteenth century, and the reasons for their proliferation lie deep in the economic history of the region. Although home-brewing was common and widespread, as elsewhere in England, the handicraft-brewer, the licensed victualler capable of producing quality ales on his own premises, was for some reason rather rare in the extreme northern counties—perhaps because, until the early nineteenth century, people were content with the more primitive form of home-brewing (a state of affairs created partly by the poor communications of previous decades), and perhaps because there was a vigorous trade in smuggled spirits, from the Isle of Man or from secret stills in the remote countryside! The rapid industrial development of the nineteenth century, especially in the Workington, Whitehaven and Barrow districts, led to a great demand for the products of brewing which could not be satisfied by the old methods, and so numerous small and medium-sized breweries appeared. There were, by the middle of the century, two in Workington, four in Whitehaven, two in Kendal, one at Egremont and three in Carlisle. Soon afterwards there were two in newly arisen Barrow, and no fewer than five in the small town of Ulverston. Some of these disappeared as larger enterprises became the rule after the 1870s.

The picture below shows an old-established brewery which survived, that of Messrs Jennings at Cockermouth, which had three malting establishments in 1887, as well as sixteen licensed houses and several cottages. The Castle Brewery (illustrated, in the background) and one malt house remain, and the company has licensed houses throughout west and central Cumberland at the present day.

The Cleator Moor brewery (above) grew up in 1875 to meet the demands of thirsty iron-workers and ore miners, but established a bonded warehouse in Whitehaven. By diversifying its business it survived when many small local breweries disappeared.

The lower picture shows the fine surviving malthouse and kiln of the Carlisle 'New' Brewery by the Caldew, late eighteenth-century structures which were altered and extended in 1865. Carlisle brewing commenced effectively in 1756 and there were four establishments by 1796, the 'Old' Brewery by the castle walls being the most important historically.

BISCUIT MANUFACTURE

Between 1750 and 1850, as road and then railway communications developed, Carlisle became a regional centre of food and drink processing, dealing in corn, bacon and seeds, and its market area overran market towns like Wigton and Brampton which accordingly lost trade and importance. This process of consolidation was undoubtedly aided by the opening of the Port Carlisle canal in 1823 (see also p96), connecting the Solway with the city itself. Jonathan Dodgson Carr (1806-84) had the foresight to purchase ground for a bakery and flourmilling business only a few yards from the canal terminus to the west of the city. Just as home-brewing at first hindered the drink industry, so home-baking, general in the region, was slowly giving way to the baking and confectionery trade. Carr, a Quaker, in achieving a breakthrough, established the birthplace of the modern biscuit industry in the north (1831).

The original oven arches (above left) are still to be seen in the 'biscuit cabin', an early structure now incorporated in the modern works of Messrs Carr, and standing about 50yd behind the frontage building shown on page 35. (This building was a bakery in the 1830s.) The rings by the arches were for resting the paddle-like long-handled shovels used by the bakery staff. The mangle-like hand machine (below left) is a 'dough break' used in the manufacture of biscuits and pastry at this early period, the dough being forced through the rollers. Nearby, in the bulk warehouse, is preserved the biscuit-cutting machine designed by Jonathan Dodgson Carr in 1849 (above). It will be seen that this machine owes a great deal, in its design, to the flatbed printing press. It should be noticed that Messrs Porter of Carlisle, the makers of this machine, won a gold medal in 1862 for a probably improved version of this device, invented by T. Holstead, confectioner of Carlisle.

LIME-BURNING

This limekiln, which can be seen near Coniston, is sited on a source of limestone which was being worked at this point in 1690. Agricultural lime was probably first used in this region in the late medieval period; the Dudley of Yanwath papers show that lime was being sold in the early seventeenth century, and Sir Patricius Curwen was using it on his estates well before 1646. It was burnt on the Fleming estate at Rydal in 1631, and some of the limestone carted there came from the band on which this Coniston kiln is situated.

This specimen is about 150 years old. From the nature of its design, it cannot be the earliest kiln. Eighteenth-century kilns were oval bowls that tapered down to the hearth where doors allowed access and the lime was raked out. The frontal arch had to be, in consequence, large enough to admit a man. Eventually it was realised that in order to remove efficiently the carbon dioxide given off in the lime-burning, a forced draught was needed, and in consequence, mid-nineteenth-century kilns were reversed in internal shape, and had necks narrower than their waists. As coal was imported in greater quantities, especially after 1700 in coastal areas and after 1819 in Westmorland (via the Lancaster Canal), so more kilns were built on large farm estates and on newly enclosed lands. Those built after 1819 are very numerous in south Westmorland, each kiln being near a small limestone quarry or digging. In the extreme east of the region, coal was obtained from the moors. Often too much lime was used by farmers reclaiming fell land 150 years ago, and much land which gave good crops is rough fell grazing once more.

POTTERY

Lakeland is not usually associated with pottery-making, which commenced in Whitehaven in 1732. There were three potteries in the Ginns in that town in 1829, the best known and most artistic being Wilkinson's. It is possible that the making of earthenware was more wide-spread, and the kiln shown above, the property of Messrs Schofield of Wetheriggs near Clifton, Westmorland, is on an old-established site. In March 1855, a Mr Tweddle advertised this pottery for sale: '... with trade in milkbowls, Cream pots, Tea pots, garden vases, Flower Pots, Brown earthenware, Chimney Tops, Solid and Hollow Bricks, Sewerage pipes, Drainage Tiles, Clay, Kilns and Machinery all Excellent'. Since then the business has been continuously in the Schofield family. The present single kiln has an open top, although if it were in a town, the Potteries-type narrow neck would be enforced to prevent smoke pollution.

Originally the clay for the Wetheriggs firm was dug locally, but better ware is now made of imported Staffordshire mixtures, worked in the clay-mixing pit shown (above). The drive is by crown gearing and line-shaft from a small diesel (originally a coal-fired) engine. The firm of Schofield have kept alive an old pattern and tradition of ornament in their production of the Westmorland salt jar (below left).

Later Woodland Industries

The term coppice literally means 'grown for cutting'. One acre of well-grown coppice was capable of producing about 10,000 poles of this size at every cutting. This was the raw material for bark tanneries, swill baskets, grommets, hoops, charcoal and bobbins. This picture was taken in the Winster Valley and illustrates a representative scene, either in southern Westmorland or in many parts of High Furness. A few bobbin and sawmills still operate, but charcoal-burning ceased between thirty and forty years ago.

COOPERAGE, HOOP-MAKING AND BARK-PEELING

The products of the woodland supplied gunpowder coopers, specimens of whose handi-work can be seen on the trolley at the former Elterwater gunpowder works. The powder kegs were bound with great lengths of hoop; the lower picture shows hoops being made at Hawkshead Field some sixty years ago. The industry itself was an old one; for a description of hoop-making see the authors' *Industrial Archaeology of the Lake Counties*, pp 171-2.

The coiling frame is on the left. The hooper is using a simple frame and wedge to split a coppice pole. Behind him is a 'mare' on which he sat to use a draw-knife to trim the roughed-out hoop strip.

Bark for the tanneries was cut in early summer when rising sap in the coppiced oak trees made the bark come off easily. The contract period for bark-peeling ran from 10 May to 5 July. This worker is engaged in 'oozing' off the bark after ringing it. The stripped oak was valuable for the fashioning of swill baskets, for gunpower charcoal and for rotproof rustic fencing.

TANNING

Early tanning was a process that might last up to fifteen months. The hides were first limed to loosen the hair, which was then scraped off on a hogback, a shaped piece of stone (see inset illustration dehiding a goatskin, 1845). The hogback illustrated below is of Penrith sandstone, 5ft x 3ft. The hides were then washed and dumped in a pit in which hen and pig manure lay. The acid counteracted the lime and the hide sinews began to swell and thicken into leather fibres. Then came a long process in which the hides were left in a succession of tannin pits, the first ones old and mellow, the last fresh and strong. This old tannery site, at Rusland in Furness, has a former manure pit and a series of rectangular vats; the one building contains a semi-circular wall, which in turn indicates the former use of a horse-gin to crush the bark. One of the crushing stones can be seen in the same building. There are also the remains of a millpond and wheelrace. In the mid-nineteenth century there were over ninety small tanneries in Lakeland, all of which needed the services of bark-peelers, bark houses for storage, and bark mills of the kind used at Rusland.

CLOG MAKING

Mr R. Brew's shop in Roper Street, Whitehaven, is one of the few cloggers' shops now left in England (top). A clogger is seen at work in the lower picture, using his hinged stock-knife to cut out the sole. A similar technique and tool were used to cut brush-stocks in Kendal in the nineteenth century. Stocks and soles originated in local woods.

The Keswick pencil industry, which had become famous by the mid-nineteenth century and which accounted for fourteen local firms in 1847, owed its origins to the nearby supplies of graphite, plumbago or 'wadd', mined in Borrowdale. The plumbago had been known from Tudor times, and in the eighteenth century it was used for hardening crucibles, for stopping rust and for fastening blue dyes. Crude blacklead pencils were also made from this mineral, and in 1765 the French metallurgist, Gabriel Jars, referred to the 'Barrowdale' mine (*sic*) as 'The famous, and I believe the only, mine known in Europe for good pencils'. Such were the restrictions, however, that locals made poor quality pencils from the rejected ore, and the later pencil manufacturers, who established a fully organised industry by about 1819, had to obtain the local plumbago via London. Although the later manufacturers—among whom the family of Banks was prominent—used waterpowered mills, the trade of pencil-making was originally a hand one involving the making of grooved blocks of fine timber, inserting the 'lead' in the grooves, and then glueing two blocks together and sawing them through into separate square pencil-units, later rounded and painted. Imported graphite was used by the 1860s.

BANKS & CO.,

Black Lead Pencil Manufacturers

To Her Majesty, the late Queen Adelaide, the King of Saxony, the King of the Belgians.

GRETA PENCIL WORKS, KESWICK, CUMBERLAND.

BANKS & Co. are the original Makers of the celebrated FIRE-PROOF LEADS, suitable for Lund's, Mordan's, Perry's, and other Pencil Cases, warranted to any size or length. Being Fireproof it is a sure test of genuine quality.

N.B.—NOTE THE FULL ADDRESS AS ABOVE.

JOSEPH BANKS, PENCIL MANUFACTURER
Keswick who died June 2nd 1860, in the
53rd YEAR OF HIS AGE.
ALSO OF ANN HIS WIFE, WHO DIED AUGUST 16
1871, AGED 60 YEARS.
ELIZABETH THE DAUGHTER OF JOSEPH & ANN BANKS
KESWICK, WHO DIED OCTr 24th 1837, AGED 1 Yr.

BOBBIN TURNING

Unlike most of the seventy-nine bobbin mills which appeared or already existed in Lakeland during the nineteenth century, those illustrated are unusual in that they were both built specifically as bobbin mills. Most of the others were converted from some other function, like cornmilling or papermaking. Oakbank Mill, Burneside, Westmorland (above), was built in 1847, and the photograph shows very clearly the separate kiln on the left with its chimney connected only by underground flue. A fine coppice drying shed is on the right; a structure of this kind very often indicates the immediate whereabouts of a long-disused bobbin mill. Stott Park bobbin mill (below) was erected in 1835 and let in February 1836, 'containing sufficient convenience and power for 24 lathes, exclusive of every other appendage requisite for Bobbin Makers'. The square-planned building on the extreme left was the first to be put up, the lathes receiving their power from a waterwheel in the rear of this building. The coppice barns were added in 1880, the square pillars—a later pattern—being distinguished from the round ones, of pre-1850 type, at Oakbank.

This picture conveys something of the appearance of the interior of a bobbin mill, the arrangement of this mill at Stott Park being typical of the industry at any time in the last century and a quarter. Underneath the roof-ridge is the line-shafting, distributing the power-drive through belting connected with lathes along each side of the shop. Smaller machines were sometimes set centrally, like the boring machine shown above (centre). This specimen, about a hundred years old, was made by the Westmorland firm of Henry Braithwaite & Sons, famous for their inventive machine-building for the bobbin industry.

Sawmills, in Lakeland as elsewhere, were often established in the vicinity of bobbin mills. This crane at Greenridge sawmill, Underbarrow, Westmorland (above) is part of a splendidly preserved establishment. The W.A. Fell lathe (below) is one of many still produced by a native woodworking machinery industry which grew up with the bobbin industry itself.

Mining and Allied Trades

This is Saltom coal pit, near Whitehaven, as it appeared 200 to 100 years ago; the drawing has been trace-copied from a faded photograph of c1864, a real treasure (loaned to the authors by Mr J. Macmillan of Hensingham).

This is the scene today. The deterioration of this industrial monument has been startling yet it was here that Cumbrian undersea mining was first commenced, with the aid of Newcomen engines, in 1731.

COALMINING

The West Cumberland coalfield is of course one of the well-known fields of the north, but it is not the only Cumbrian locality in which mining has been pursued. The small northern Cumberland field east of Carlisle was worked extensively (chiefly in the parishes of Midgeholme, Hayton and Geltsdale) in the eighteenth and nineteenth centuries, and some archaeological remains may still be seen there. Coal has been traditionally dug on the moors near Caldbeck and at Kaber, Hartley, Stainmore and Barbon in Westmorland. The pictures in this section, however, deal with a number of the more striking West Cumberland monuments and scenes relative to coalmining.

Most of the working areas of this field have been within a few miles of the towns of Whitehaven, Workington and Maryport; indeed, the most spectacular growth of the industry took place in the seventeenth and eighteenth centuries in what is now the borough of Whitehaven. Each of these towns owes its rise and growth, in large measure, to the flourishing coal trade with Ireland which was carried on under the hegemony of the Lowther, Christian, Senhouse and Fletcher families. This domination by a few families is one striking feature of local coalmining history; another such feature is the high capitalisation and technically advanced exploitation of a few very large collieries situated close to the sea, as at Whitehaven; another is the vast extent of undersea mining that has been pursued; another is the remarkable and sometimes bizarre colliery architecture that is still to be seen in the field. although town developers now show an inclination to sweep it away.

Long before the age of town redevelopment, a variety of agencies tended to treat industrial monuments with contempt—or was this caused by a sense of unease, or even conscience, engendered by the dirt, misery and exploitation they sometimes represented? Whatever the case, there is no justification for simply sweeping them away; they are uniquely valuable as reminders of the good and evil in the past. Had it been possible to preserve Saltom pit (opposite) in something like its original shape, the country would have had a unique specimen of an eighteenth-century pit site, the work of one of the leading mining engineers of that age, Carlisle Spedding, who first applied the Newcomen engine to extensive undersea mining (1731).

The Lowthers and the Curwens had a taste for striking colliery architecture, as is demonstrated on pages 52 and 54. Their taste had more than a hint of industrial feudalism about it, and this was all too much in keeping with the Lowther rule over the Whitehaven district. But it was also in keeping with the spirit of the period 1830-50, when Jane and Wellington pits were designed.

Although it was the brain-child of Henry Curwen (1843-4), Jane pit, with its turrets and keep-like engine house, looks like a transplanted fragment of baronial hall. This photograph is a reproduction of a print at least 100 years old, which reveals the former position of the flywheel and pumping gear. Today we can see that Jane pit has suffered far less than Saltom pit did in the course of a century; indeed, the Workington Corporation is now actively interested in the preservation of the site, which is at NGR 995277. Although the flywheel and headstocks have now gone, the scene has altered little.

(Opposite above) This well-preserved Guibal fan housing of c1862 once contained a 36ft wooden fan that extracted foul air from Duke Pit, Whitehaven. It was unexpectedly revealed in 1969 and is to be preserved by the Whitehaven Civic Society.

At nearby William Pit, sunk in 1810, a battery of ninety-one brickwork ovens reveals another activity of local mining—that of coke manufacture. The lower picture is a view into a beehive oven constructed in 1881. These were the last to be built in Cumberland on the Breckon and Dixon design of 1858, which used the previously wasted volatiles to raise steam.

The sinking of Wellington pit, Whitehaven, was begun in 1840 and completed in 1845. Meanwhile the architect Sydney Smirke, brother of the designer of the British Museum, had surrounded the pit site (on the south side of Whitehaven harbour) with masonry. Now only the famous 'candlestick' chimney (background) remains. The pit site, which has recently been cleared and landscaped, once presented the stark but impressive appearance shown in the picture, trace-copied by M. Davies-Shiel from a photograph of 11 May 1911. Whitehaven Castle (below), on the south side of the town proper, seems to have provided the inspiration for the engine house (centre, between the chimneys).

Token coinage was commonly issued by industrial enterprises in the late eighteenth century. The specimen shown here, (by courtesy of Mrs Gordon Workington—this one may have been used as a lamp token in the nineteenth century) with its obverse, depicts an atmospheric engine in use for winding at Greysouthen near Workington (pronounced Greysoon), where, in 1781, pits were being worked by both Sir James Lowther and Messrs Cookson of Little Clifton. William Brown's 1769 list of atmospheric engines shows that one was in use at Greysouthen in that year.

The unpretentious-seeming outhouse to an early nineteenth-century cottage at Wreah, Hensingham, is almost certainly the former office of one of Lord Lonsdale's smaller pits.

The physically small Cumberland coalfield lay at the heart of a clearly marked industrial zone which now seems to have little in common with the better-known parts of the Lake Counties. A separate world and way of life had been created by industrialism in this re- mote coastal strip, even though, socially, this district was very much part of Cumbrian thought and tradition. Yet much of the transformation has been very recent. The hilly territory shown in the background of this photograph—the Pica district 2 miles inland from Lowca and Moresby—lay comparatively untouched a century ago, with a few small col- lieries hidden behind its hedgerows. The miners' terraces of Pica, on the skyline, had not appeared. The nearby industrial village of Distington (pronounced Dissington) was still a largely rural place, with cornmill, sawmill, brewery and limekilns. In 1879 the Cleator & Workington Junction Railway was opened to carry iron ore up to the Workington and Dis- tington furnaces, and the remains of one of the bridges can be seen up the road; the line (closed since 1963), served the area long after the iron ore mines a few miles south, had been worked out. The development of Dyan, Oatlands and Castlerigg collieries also played a part in transforming this local landscape, and the miners' rows were built follow- ing this. These collieries, too, are abandoned, and the pit-hills are being absorbed slowly into the landscape as were the smaller spoilheaps of the eighteenth-century pits.

LEAD AND COPPER MINING

Fortunately, non-ferrous mining, unlike quarrying, has not left many obtrusive marks on the Lakeland scene, and only in one or two places has it left extensive waste, dereliction and a legacy of eyesores. Consequently the visitor is often unaware of the extent to which it has been carried on during the last four centuries. Yet there is hardly a major part of the mountainous area that does not carry some traces of mining activity.

There are three main mining areas in Lakeland, which are related, for convenience, to the geological formations in which they occur. Immediately to the west and north of Keswick is the mining area of the Skiddaw slates, containing an economically and historically important group of mines, mainly lead and copper. The copper-lead workings in the vicinity of the Newlands Valley, which belong to this group, were exploited by the Company of Mines Royal in the sixteenth century, and a few traces of their activity can still be seen. A second mining area, situated on the Borrowdale Volcanic Series, stretches from south-west Cumberland to the Ullswater locality and the edge of the Vale of Eden; this, in its southern extremity, includes the former Coniston and Tilberthwaite copper mines and the famous Greenside lead mine near the northern side of Ullswater. A third mining area, not so easy to distinguish in terms of a single rock formation but technically in the Skiddaw slates, is to be found on the eastern side of that mountain and around the lower skirts of its neighbour, Blencathra, or further east and north-east in the valley of the River Caldew. This latter locality, which embraces Carrock Fell, has igneous intrusions and is famous thereby for the variety of its minerals. These include wolfram (ore of tungsten), galena or lead sulphide, blende (the black zinc sulphide), barytes or crude barium sulphate (used in paint manufacture, dyeing and a variety of other industrial processes), and a mineral called scheelite which becomes fluorescent under ultra-violet light. The visitor will find traces of water courses, washing plant, wheel pits, and of course shafts and workings. Generally speaking, the remains are those of plant used in the nineteenth century. Some are decidedly scanty, on the surface of the ground at least. Yet there is immense fascination in the reconstruction of these former mining sites.

This view of Thornthwaite Lead Mine, Bassenthwaite, was photographed in 1902, with the camera pointing northwards along the main road from Keswick to Cockermouth. The scene is now largely rural.

Power was provided through a 75in Pelton wheel of 45hp, the water descending Ladstock Beck from a million gallon reservoir 500ft above. Part of a large penstock can be seen on the left hand side of the photograph. Sections of this supply pipe remain today at about NGR 219252. The pitbank platform is now a garage, and considerable quantities of crushed material extend to the east of the road. The mine employed over 90 men during its 35 years of life, and an average of over £5,000 worth of lead and zinc concentrates was sold annually by its owners.

The eye trained to look out for early iron-smelting traces can also discern those left by copper-smelting. Genuinely old accumulations of slag, like the scoriae shown on page 8, should be sharply distinguishable from much more recent material. These large cones of copper slag were left by a smelt mill set up at Coniston about 1894, not far from the present Coppermines Youth Hostel. The mill was destroyed a year or two later. Generally speaking, the Lakeland mining firms of the last century left very little mechanical gear behind them. The central gearing of this horse gin at Tilberthwaite is an exception. It is fairly modern, and shows that horse traction might be a useful standby at a remote spot, even in the twentieth century.

Early in this century, the great and productive Greenside lead mine was described by M. J. B. Baddeley as 'the one blot on the otherwise almost perfect loveliness' of the Patterdale locality. Completely equipped when it was closed in 1962, it is now largely dismantled and much less in evidence. Two centuries old, it was the first metalliferous mine in England to use electric haulage (1891). The extensive slate-quarrying of Lakeland has had a greater effect on the landscape than has mining. The Honister slate quarries were in operation in the mid-eighteenth century and their green slate, like that of Coniston and Tilberthwaite, was in great demand, especially when roads improved. It is still worked at all these places and is prized for ornamental purposes and durability.

This view will be familiar to many visitors to the Coppermines Youth Hostel at Coniston; the latter, indeed, has taken over the former office and manager's cottage belonging to the mines themselves. About ninety years ago this was a scene of great activity with, to the right of the valley causeway, extensive jigging plant driven by waterpower, together with settling tanks and spoil heaps. The remains of buildings at the near bend of the track are those of the Electrolytic Copper Company's works of c1908, closed soon after World War I. Sorting of the ore, by means of hand-picking and the use of iron gratings, took place in an area to the right of the picture, and the ore and veinstone were brought out of the hillside to its immediate left, at a point near the stream, and carried by waggonway across the foot of the slope on which the cameraman is standing. The building complex at the left foot of the slope served several purposes over time. The wheelpit visible on the extreme left-hand side was constructed about 1874 to house a 32ft diameter wheel which drove three circular saws in the adjacent mines joiners' shop, its headrace having been cut about 1848 for a smaller wheel. Then, after the closure of the mines in the 1880s, a turbine shed was built on the site (above) for the cutting of slate.

This was not merely a mining site, but an industrial colony. In the distance, on the left-hand side of the valley, is a row of miners' houses which remain as a reminder of the men who worked here. Some of them were immigrants from the Alston district.

61

VALUABLE MINING PROPERTY.

THE WELL-KNOWN

CONISTON AND TILBERTHWAITE COPPER MINES,

IN NORTH LANCASHIRE.

MESSRS. T. M. FISHER SONS & Co.

ARE INSTRUCTED TO SELL AS A GOING CONCERN,

AT THE CLARENCE HOTEL, SPRING GARDENS, MANCHESTER,

ON TUESDAY, THE 3RD OF AUGUST, 1875,

At 4 for 5 o'clock in the Afternoon, in one or more Lots as may be decided upon, subject to Conditions of Sale to be then produced.

ALL THOSE VALUABLE AND EXTENSIVE

MINING PROPERTIES,

KNOWN AS THE CONISTON AND TILBERTHWAITE COPPER MINES, WITH

41 FREEHOLD HOUSES, COPPER STATION, 13 LEASEHOLD COTTAGES,

And all the BUILDINGS, MACHINERY, & PLANT.

The water power is almost unlimited, levels having been driven up into the two mountain tarns called **Levers Water** and **Low Water**, from which, in addition to the mountain streams, large supplies of water are drawn. No steam power is required, and the only coals used are at the Smiths' Shops and the Offices.

The present lease of the Coniston Sett expires in 1880, the Royalty is $\frac{1}{15}$th, and a renewal of the Lease on the same terms can be obtained. The only surface rent payable is £9 a year for the Land the Copper Station is built upon, and the road to it.

The TILBERTHWAITE ROYALTY comprises a large area adjoining to Coniston, the deep level has been driven 1080 yards, and unwaters a large district, one lode only has been partially opened on, there are three other lodes in a short distance, and there is no doubt large returns will be made from this Mine. There is also a vein of Slate rock of good quality near the level mouth, for which offers to work have recently been made. The supply of water here is also most ample.

These Mines are held on lease of which ten years are unexpired, at a minimum rent of £60 merging in a Royalty of $\frac{1}{18}$th.

These great mines were finally destroyed not by the exhaustion of the copper veins, but by the success of the Rio Tinto mines, the disappearance of wooden vessels (which used copper sheathing) from the seas, and competition from Chile. This is part of a sale advertisement of 3 August 1875.

SPADE MANUFACTURE

The establishment of spade forges took place in the region in the mid-eighteenth century, reflecting both the development of agriculture and industry. The spades were used in mining as well as farming. On the whole, however, the stimulus seems to have come from iron-mining, and these establishments, at Cleator (below) and Lowick Green, Furness (above) were of course fairly near haematite areas, although other forges at Dalston and near Cockermouth must have relied heavily on more general markets. The main forge house at Cleator, shown here, had a 30ft waterwheel on the side nearest the camera; evidently the open archway left a space for the pitring which powered the hammer. The tailrace, now filled in, came out towards the camera. (See also page 87 for further notes on this industry.)

GUNPOWDER MANUFACTURE

The picture below shows the former manager's office of the Gatebeck gunpowder works, operative about a century ago, and situated about 5 miles south-east of Kendal. Such sites were usually extensive, accommodating a series of waterpowered processes, which had to be separated to minimise the danger of 'sympathetic' explosions. Today the seven gunpowder works sites of Lakeland consist of large wasteland or woodland tracts, with only a few indicative remains or traces; the best preserved example is that at Elterwater, Great Langdale, which has been converted into a holiday centre with chalets. Gatebeck was the last to close, in 1937, but most of the site has recently been bulldozed flat.

The first of the gunpowder works was built at Sedgwick, south of Kendal on the river Kent, in 1764, to be followed by that at nearby Basingill (1790) and Lowwood in Furness in 1799. In the nineteenth century four more plants followed: one in the beautiful setting of Elterwater (1824), Gatebeck, New Sedgwick and Black Beck, the latter another site in rural Furness (1860). Between them these works supplied the country with the bulk of its black

blasting-powder, the regional market for which appears to have provided the original stimulus to the appearance of these firms. A man named Michael Nolon was killed at the Coniston mines using gunpowder in 1693.

There were of course other important reasons why the industry became concentrated in part of Lakeland. Abundant waterpower was of course essential, for production called for a series of powered operations. Charcoal, a main ingredient of gunpowder, was a product of the local coppice woods, although only the charcoal of specific trees was used: juniper or savin, silver birch and alder. Again, the extensive ground accommodation was provided by shelving territory in the less cultivatable riverbank areas. Again, most of the sites were fairly near cheap water transport.

The old method of charcoal-burning did not result in a clean enough product for gunpowder-making, and so the charcoal was burnt in retorts of a kind invented by a well-known Lakeland resident, Bishop Watson, in the eighteenth century. One of these retorts can be seen at Gatebeck, serving as a gatepost (opposite). The initials of the owner of the works, John Wakefield, can be seen on the office building. The illustration below shows a scene at Elterwater, in fact the site of the No 2 Incorporating Mill of the works there. The circular pieces of stone are bedstones upon which the heavy paired limestone runners rotated on a principle identical to that shown on page 25 above (the crushing rollers at Burneside papermill). Once the pure charcoal, sulphur and saltpetre were powdered and mixed in the correct proportions, they had to be incorporated; that is, ground together under heavy pressure so that the ingredients were inextricably mixed even in the smallest of grains. The roller mechanism of the mill in the foreground was suspended, the heavy stones running about 2in above the 'green charge' of semi-prepared powder. The original mill was built about 1824.

Gunpowder barrels from Lowwood (closed 1934) were transferred to Haverthwaite station by means of three special 1m gauge vans. The picture at the top of the opposite page shows the unusual type of wheel springing. Each van had wooden buffers, was pulled up the slope by one horse (with copper horseshoes) which then made its own way back to the stables. The van, once emptied, was brought down by the vanman who stood on his seat with one foot on the brake, holding on by the handle shown. Two open trucks remain on the site. The last remaining saltpetre boiling pan, 11ft by 7ft (opposite below) lies to the south of the office block at Lowwood. At Elterwater there is a covered walk-way leading to the furnace doorways for each of the three saltpetre pots that were used there. Apart from these two locations no other boiling apparatus remains in Lakeland.

IRON MINING

The air photograph (right) (Crown Copyright) gives a powerful impression of the pitted and fissured surface of the Cleator Moor area, West Cumberland, the effect of the haematite iron ore mining which was at its peak about a century ago, and which terminated about 1916. Haematite, which had been known and used in small quantities for several centuries, became especially valuable in the mid-nineteenth century because of its use to the Bessemer steelmaker. It is non-phosphoric, a quality essential to the Bessemer process, and it is also exceedingly rich, containing between 54 per cent and 66 per cent metallic iron, one variety being the bizarre or beautiful kidney ore, with its lustrous lobes. It was found in great cavities in the carboniferous limestone, and the removal of these 'sops' of iron ore leaves gaping holes in the landscape like quarries, surrounded by broken ground, tips and the remains of buildings.

The neatly laid-out town of Cleator Moor (below left) began to appear in the 1840s on the former common land of the parish of Cleator, the old village of which can be seen at the top of the photograph (left side). By the 1860s and 1870s Cleator Moor had taken the shape seen here and was a community almost entirely composed of iron ore miners, often Irish, and their families, with schools, churches, chapels and public houses, not to mention a small brewery which met growing market demands. These items of social history are mentioned here because the study of technological history cannot be profitably pursued without taking into account the human aspect, and the formation of communities is a consequence of industrial development. The iron mines were an integral part of this community existence, and a way of life disappeared when they closed.

It is estimated that about five million tons of ore were extracted from the area of landscape seen here in the photograph, the output reaching a peak in the 1880s and declining more or less steadily thereafter. Ore had been extracted in this locality in the eighteenth century and exported to the furnaces of the famous Carron Company of Scotland; indeed, this company operated one of the mines at Jacktrees (mid-left on the picture) in the nineteenth century also.

The major instrument in the development of this district, as of its 'opposite number' in Furness, was the railway system which was laid to carry away the ore in the 1850s and 1860s—the original Whitehaven, Cleator & Egremont line, as it was then known, can be seen in the lower central portion of the photograph. The Furness Railway played a similar part in its own ironfield, where the results, and the effects upon the scenery, were also closely comparable. The tracks or beds of numerous branch railway lines can be traced here, and because of the close proximity of some of the larger mines, the countryside became a maze of waggonways and footpaths. Field boundaries disappeared, while the River Keekle, which can be followed along the upper central area of the photograph, was encased in a concrete 'trough' as it passed Moor Row Junction (extreme right, centre), this in order that the Crossfield Iron Company could mine beneath it.

Most of the ore was mined underground and raised up shafts, the permanent winding shafts being sunk through the solid limestone at the edge of a 'sop' wherever possible. The solid haematite was removed in 'slices' by a form of pillar-and-stall working, the surface or upper ground being allowed to subside or collapse. But at Todholes (left centre), the ore was won by open-cast or quarry working.

Ullcoats iron mine, near Egremont, was in operation until 1969. Like the great mine at Hodbarrow (pp 72-3), it was a continuation of a tradition, and also a reminder of a past way of life which flourished before it became customary (from the 1880s) to bring haematite ore from Spain and North Africa. Such are the caprices of economic life that the mines have been closed when some ore yet remains unworked, and a nearby company, at Haile Moor, has obtained extraction rights in the Ullcoats and Florence mineworkings. The above picture shows well the impressive scenic background to much of Cumberland industry.

The upper picture shows Diamond haematite pit, near Lindal-in-Furness, as it appeared in about 1907, complete with railway line, substantial headstocks for the winding gear, boiler chimney and engine house. As is shown in the lower picture, recently taken, the engine house (rather unusually for this locality) has been converted to other uses, but has otherwise remained unscathed but for the insertion of doorways at the near end. Comparatively few complete pithead structures remain in the Furness and Cumberland ironfields, and the visitor, accordingly, can have little clear notion of the smoking chimneys, noisy engines, and creaking trucks that were once a commonplace beyond almost every hedge and at the end of every lane. In a number of instances, the sites of large and once busily occupied pits have disappeared in the undergrowth, with hardly a sign that they ever existed.

HODBARROW IRON MINE

This is a view of the remarkable Hodbarrow, south-west Cumberland, ironmining site, at which mining ceased as recently as 1968. Historically one of the most important and productive haematite mines in the world, Hodbarrow began large-scale extraction in the 1860s, and so had over a century of operation. Tiny quantities of ore may have been taken away from the locality in the seventeenth century, however, by Hudleston of Millom.

This view was taken from the engine platform of the No 8 Cornish beam-engine house, looking westwards along the original coastline to the Moorbank headstock and the village of Haverigg. A very large iron-ore deposit was discovered below ground in the area to the right of the picture, and mining began in 1880. Soon afterwards, in order to counteract coastal erosion, a timber barrier was erected on the seaward side (see the authors' *Industrial Archaeology of the Lake Counties*, p129). Further ore was found in the direction of the seabed, however, and a new permanent wall, the Inner Barrier, was made in 1888-9. It had an outer face of stone and concrete curved to deflect wave thrusts, and was supported by a heavy mass-work foundation and a deep clay embankment; but the wall, seen here in its partially collapsed state, was undermined as the ore was taken from beneath, and in 1905 the skilfully constructed Outer Barrier was made to protect the extended workings and, although all pumping ceased in 1968, this great piece of engineering still keeps the sea out.

Until their recent destruction, Hodbarrow's Cornish beam-engines were objects of admiration to students of engineering from all over England, and were the last local survivors of a hardy and powerful race, designed to pump water, sand and pebbles from pit bottom. This picture shows the beam and housing of the engine at Number 10 shaft (1968), with (left) the embossed seal used by the Hodbarrow Mining Company, depicting one of the engine houses as shown in the main picture. This engine, which had on its beam the legend 'Williams, Perran Foundry Co., Cornwall 1878', continued to work until 1962, after having seen service at the nearby Annie Lowther shaft. It was of $147\frac{1}{2}$ horsepower and had a 10ft stroke. The heavy studded rods were counterbalanced at the surface, and the narrower rod behind worked the air pump in the external condenser. The boiler house chimney is on the right.

Hodbarrow shipped out some of its ore in small coastal vessels to Germany and other continental countries. The lighthouse on the site, which thus had a purpose, dates from about 1879. These side-tipping pier wagons (below) earlier had wooden containers of c1890, the chassis frames being 'original'.

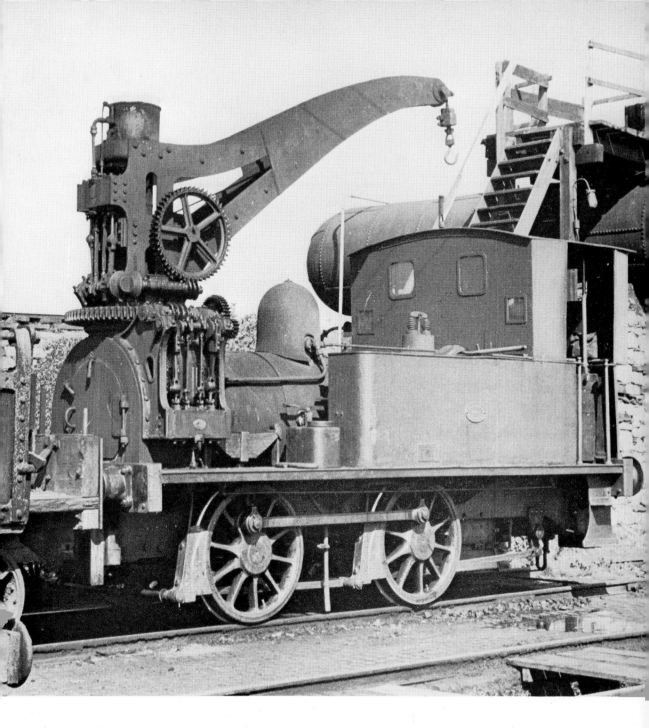

This 0-4-0 Hodbarrow locomotive, besides being locally famous, is known to railway enthusiasts throughout the country. 'Snipey' was built by the Nielson Company, Glasgow, in 1890 as No 4004, and is a unique mixture of tank engine and mobile crane, weighing 19 tons altogether. When the mine was closed, this engine went into the Morris industrial locomotive collection at Lytham St Annes.

Iron Manufacture

Following the early and primitive forms of iron-smelting described on page 9, the Lakeland iron industry became progressively more elaborate in the seventeenth and eighteenth centuries. As blast furnaces were erected, so increasing quantities of charcoal were consumed, and several eighteenth-century ironmaking sites in the region still have the great storage barns which were used to house the full sacks of charcoal for charging the nearby furnace during a blast lasting several weeks. This barn at the site of Nibthwaite furnace and forge (1736) is almost certainly the oldest specimen of its type in the region, and part of the masonry may be late medieval.

With the new cold-blast furnaces went separate finery and chafery forges, often situated at a distance from the furnaces which produced supplies of pig iron for working into bar iron at the forges. The finery forge at Stony Hazel in the Rusland valley is the only complete specimen of its type known to remain in the British Isles and was built in 1718, only about seven years after the first local blast furnace at Backbarrow. The pictures opposite show the Stony Hazel site before clearance, on 17 August 1968 (above), and after careful clearance, at an interval of rather over a year (below). There is a very clearly marked wheel pit and dam, but, more strikingly, the site was found to contain the base for the forge hammer, the upright tree trunk base for the anvil, and even the working end of a helve hammer head. The hearth has been excavated and is almost complete.

The clearance and scrutiny of this site was undertaken by the authors and others working in collaboration with the Historical Metallurgy Group and the Cumberland and Westmor-

land Antiquarian and Archaeological Society. Like all other historic or archaeological sites, it should be respected; interference and trespass by well-meaning enthusiasts can lead to untold harm. Visits can be arranged for groups.

John Wilkinson, ironmaster, one of the 'general staff' of the Industrial Revolution of the eighteenth century, had numerous associations with Lakeland. His father, Isaac, worked in the Cumberland iron industry from about 1728, in which year John seems to have been born. At some time in the following ten years Isaac became chief caster or 'potfounder' to the Backbarrow Iron Company and resided at the house known as Bare Syke in Backbarrow village, which can still be seen. There is little or no real proof that John Wilkinson helped him regularly, if at all, in the work of casting, as a popular story claims, and not much real evidence relating to John's activities at Wilson House, Cartmel, where Isaac moved after 1748. But it is known that in 1753 the father set up business as an ironmaster in Bersham near Wrexham, and that John was there not long after, soon to establish his own claims to fame. About 1778-9 John purchased the Castlehead estate near Grange-over-Sands, and at that time began experiments with peat smelting at Wilson House, experiments which have formerly been thought to belong to the 1750s. It need not surprise us, therefore, that this Wilkinson iron pipe (right), part of a barn at Wilson House Farm, is dated 1784. It was typical of this remarkable man that he should have an iron monument, to be seen at Lindale-in-Cartmel today, with its flamboyant inscription. But this is probably less untruthful than some of the local legends concerning him.

The Backbarrow furnace, around which Isaac Wilkinson worked over two hundred years ago, remained operative from 1711 to 1964, when the modernised plant ceased production. The Charcoal Iron Company of recent times established a high reputation for its coke-smelted pig iron, three types of which are indicated on the above marking irons: 'Leven', 'Valley' and 'Anglo-Swedish Valley'. The furnace-charging barrows (below) have a shape resembling that of early specimens in the Forest of Dean.

The original Newland furnace was built about 1748, and the founding company, the Newland Company, was as important as the Backbarrow partnership in the history of the northern iron trade. The furnace was rebuilt about 1770, and continued to work until 1891. The top picture was taken not long after it had been blown out. Thorough dismantling took place in 1903 but some buildings remain, as the recent photograph shows (below). The fine charcoal barn is still visible in the background.

This picture shows the stack of the Backbarrow furnace as it was after reconstruction in 1870, although a double-skinned water-circulating steel furnace was installed in 1963, thus extending the tradition of continuous iron-making on this historic spot. Even the original furnace of 1711 was preceded by a bloomsmithy of 1685 on 'the piece of ground now occupied by the Backbarrow Ironworks'.

Now that ironmaking has at last ceased at Backbarrow, steps are being taken to preserve any remaining masonry of the earlier furnace stacks, which were less than half as high as the one shown here (105ft). The most striking curio from the time of the first blast furnace is undoubtedly the original furnace lintel, marked '1711 IM WR SC', the initials standing for those of three of the four partners, John Machell, William Rawlinson and Stephen Crossfield. The fourth was John Olivant of Penrith.

When the furnace was reconstructed in 1870, a larger inscribed lintel was placed over the furnace mouth. This is the one shown in the picture above; it will be noticed that the 1711 legend is repeated, but that a star has been added centrally, with, on the right, the initials of the firm of Harrison, Ainslie and Co, and the date 1870. Between 1870 and 1926 the furnace still used charcoal, and it continued to work by a cold air blast. Iron blowing cylinders were, however, supplied to the firm by John Wilkinson in 1779. The furnace used prodigious quantities of charcoal; 'An enormous supply is required', lamented the *Westmorland Gazette* of 1 October 1898, pointing to the firm's difficulties in obtaining fuel. But the cold-blast iron was of excellent quality, and the quarrymen's bars produced by this works were sought for many miles around.

The picture of the hearth, above, shows the air ring, an unconnected tuyère, the slag taphole to the left, and the pig stamps, already illustrated on page 79, hanging on the right. Until quite recent years the older of the two lintels was clamped into the back of the furnace stack. It is now carefully preserved by the owners.

The development of the iron industry led to the establishment of numerous ports and landing places, like this wharf (above) near Duddon Bridge, probably used by the Duddon ironworks from the eighteenth century (NGR 202878), together with Lady Hall Marsh and other places. The nineteenth-century ironworks quay at Borwick Rails (below), serving the Millom ironworks, affords a complete contrast. Interestingly enough, this site, too, was used as a landing point by the Duddon Company's vessels in the 1750s.

The Millom Ironworks of the Cumberland Iron Mining & Smelting Company helped to bring into being the mushroom industrial town of Millom. The plant was of course closely connected with the Hodbarrow mine, and when the ironworks company was incorporated in 1865, it was hoped that the entire output of the mine would be smelted locally. The work commenced with two furnaces in September 1867, and the firm established a reputation for haematite pig iron of exceptionally high quality. After remaining independent of each other for nearly a century, the mining and smelting companies finally merged; but the ironworks, like the mine, now stands derelict and is already entering the realm of industrial archaeology.

THE WORK OF THE FOUNDER AND ENGINEER

As the uses of metal multiplied and spread with the building of works, railways and docks, so numerous foundries were established in Cumbrian towns. The bollards here shown are typical of their art and are of mid-nineteenth century vintage. That on the top left, at Maryport harbour, was made by J. & W. Pearson of that town, and that on the top right by another Maryport foundry, that of Andrew Henderson. The Whitehaven specimen (below left) is dated 1860, and could have been made by one of at least three foundries in that port. Messrs Stout's foundry at Newtown, Whitehaven, on the site of an earlier works, remains to represent the skills of the foundryman. There was a foundry on this site in 1815.

Haematite iron ore had certain secondary uses, as a form of paint or as an annealing element in foundry processes. The upper picture shows the remains of top-runner crushers of the former Warton & Silverdale Paint Mill (c1880), used to prepare iron ore for use as reddle or red paint, in those days put on farm buildings or Furness Railway wagons and vans. The annealing ore works at Lindal-in-Furness (below) still supply a product which is utilised to give a strong 'skin' to foundry castings.

Spades found full employment in all the activities described in the last nineteen pages, and we have seen that spade forges (p63) grew up in consequence. The manufacture of spades, shovels and edge-tools generally is partly manual craftsmanship and partly light engineering or forge work. The earliest known clear reference to edge-tools in Lakeland relates to a sickle mill in Staveley in 1689. Eventually over ten sickle mills and fifteen spade forges were in operation; four of the latter are known to have begun between 1756 and 1782, and most of the others appear to belong to that period. (Cf the authors' *Industrial Archaeology of the Lake Counties*, p100, and also pp47-9.) An indenture in the Leconfield MSS at Cockermouth Castle states that in 1756 John Bartholomew was to be apprenticed for five years as a 'spade plaiter and finisher at Cleator Plaiting Forge'. Dalston forge is believed to have commenced work in the same year.

The spades shown above, from left to right, are as follows: bell-mouth shovel, Cleator Forge (J. Lindow, c1860); shovel, c1885, Cleator Forge; railway fireman's shovel, Bridgefoot Forge, near Workington; large Cleator Forge bell-mouth, S. & J. Lindow, c 1930; and on the floor, hedge-slasher made by Cowan & Sons of Dalston forge, near Carlisle. Below: close-up of the name-stamp on the 1885 shovel (second from left).

THE LOWCA ENGINEERING COMPANY, LIMITED,

Lowca Engine Works, Whitehaven, England.

CLASS Bb.

FLETCHER'S "PATENT" TANK LOCOMOTIVE ENGINE FOR NARROW GAUGES.

This Engine is designed for use where the curves are easy, and a long wheel base is in consequence admissible, securing greater steadiness than can be obtained with Engines in which the wheel base is short and the firebox overhangs the driving axle.

The Cylinders are placed outside, and the driving axle is situated behind the firebox instead of before it. The eccentrics which give motion to the slide valves are put upon the leading or front axle instead of the driving one, and a peculiar arrangement of link motion employed.

One of these Engines, with 8-inch cylinders, has been some years at work on a railway, 2ft. 3in. gauge, in North Wales, for the conveyance of minerals and passengers. Up gradients of 1 in 75 and 1 in 66 (the latter half a mile long) its usual load is 33 tons, at a speed of 18 miles an hour.

Dimensions and Prices for Gauges under 3½ft.

Code Word.	Size of Cylinder.	Length of Stroke.	Area of Firegrate.	No. of Tubes.	Diameter of Tubes.	Size of Wheels.	Wheel Centres.	Size of Injector.	Diameter of Boiler.	Length of Boiler Barrel.	Gauge of Rails.	Aproximate Weight when Empty.	Nett Cash Price.
	In.	In.	Ft.		In.	Ft. In.	Ft. In.	No.	Ft. In.	Ft. In.	Ft. In.	Tons.	
Benbow	8	16	4	73	1½	2 6	6 6	4	2 6¾	4 9	2 3 to	8½	£650
Barbel	9	16	4¾	78	1½	2 9	7 0	4	2 9	5 3	3 6	9½	£760
Bulbul	10	20	6	110	1½	3 0	8 0	5	3 0	6 0	3 0 to 3 6	11	£860

The above is from a catalogue item of 1860. The original Lowca works is believed to have been founded in 1763 to make brass cannons for local merchant vessels. A more certain date, however, is 1799 when the inventor Adam Heslop formed a partnership with Stead, Johnson & Millward to make Heslop steam engines and iron gear. This firm was followed at the site by Tulk & Ley (1830), who between 1840 and 1845 built locomotives for the Maryport & Carlisle Railway. In 1857, Fletcher Jennings & Co took over the works and remained in production until 1884, making light locomotives for collieries, ironworks and iron mines.

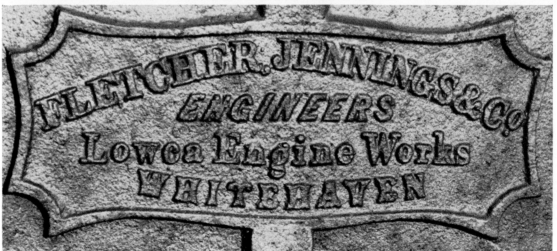

This Lowca-made locomotive now works on the Talyllyn Railway. *Dolgoch* (1866) is an 0-4-0 well tank with 2ft 3in gauge, unusual valve gear, and a long wheelbase. Another, *Talyllyn*, was built in 1864 but rebuilt later, a trailing axle being added at Lowca in 1867. Cumberland's most famous engineers (iron label, below) built locomotives until 1884; then, after changes of ownership, the Lowca works closed down in 1921, the equipment being sold in April 1926. The site now lies buried under a colliery tip near the shore at Parton, just north of Whitehaven.

Although improved land drainage led to some problems for waterpower users, steampower was not often employed in this area. Accordingly, the fascinating if rust-covered shape of some Victorian steam engine is only occasionally encountered in Lakeland mills and works. This single-cylinder engine was installed in the Stott Park bobbin mill, Finsthwaite, in 1880 to supplement a turbine in dry periods. One of three that still remain today, it was made at the ironworks of William Bradley & Sons, Brighouse. This specimen developed a mere 10hp, and was so greedy of fuel that its working life was very short.

The Stott Park enterprise had previously installed a small Williamson-type turbine (as early as 1858), and a second turbine was set up at the works about 1890. This lapse into the use of steam was quite exceptional, as is demonstrated on the following pages.

TURBINES IN LAKELAND

A turbine is essentially a perfect waterwheel of high performance, completely enclosed and with no power wastage through spilling or the bubbling of air, or counter-currents at the base of the wheel. Although there were numerous turbine inventions in the early nineteenth century, Fourneyron, about 1827, is regarded as the real originator of the modern turbine. After several devices had been put on the market, Professor Thomson of Queens College, Belfast, invented one which proved to be highly suitable to Lakeland conditions, namely the vortex wheel, which received water at the circumference and delivered it at the centre. It was designed locally for a wide range of heads and powers. In the year 1856, soon after the invention was patented, Williamson Bros of Kendal began to make these machines at the Canal Iron Works. They were about 75 per cent efficient as a rule.

This enterprising firm, erstwhile agricultural engineers, found a satisfactory market in a district which was accustomed to waterpower, and by 1881 when Gilbert Gilkes took over, 502 turbines had been sold, many of them in Lakeland. Under Gilkes' leadership new designs were added, including those of Pelton wheels and Francis turbines, and the subsequent sales drive ensured that almost every Lakeland mill, mine, quarry, public power company, farm and hotel had its own turbine by about 1940, when the firm of Gilbert Gilkes & Gordon had sold over 6,000 both at home and abroad. The firm came to specialise in low fall/large volume machines for its wider markets, while among the more important customers locally was the London Lead Company, with its famous mines on Alston Moor. By 1940 well over 40,000bhp was in use in wheels and turbines in the Lake Counties.

Orders too small for Gilkes to execute were given to a Staveley man, W. H. Storey who, self-taught, built 75 small Francis and Pelton turbines between 1924 and 1958. His major achievement was to design and build the entire turbine and generator plant to provide light and power to Salcombe in Devon in 1928. At least two machines built by him are still working locally, and he specialised in the manufacture of small model turbines for demonstration purposes. Casings were cast for him by Messrs Gilkes or other local millwrights or engineers, but he cast and machined everything else. Such self-employed men played a not inconsiderable part in supplying many users with private generating plants before widespread public supplies entered rural Lakeland in the 1940s. It may be no accident, however, that the advent of the first public electricity supply firm, the Keswick Electric Light & Power Company (1888) took place in a Lakeland environment, using waterpower exclusively. Messrs Gilbert Gilkes & Gordon exercised by 1936 what was virtually a monopoly of small and medium sized turbines made in the United Kingdom although another firm, Wright, Heaps & Westwood, operated in Kendal for a time.

It has been so thoroughly habitual to regard water as a somewhat dated prime mover in the history of the English Industrial Revolution, that historians of economic development have overlooked this important adaptation of waterpower in a relatively remote district.

The picture above shows the historic No 1 vortex turbine invented by Professor John Thomson and made by Messrs Williamson at Canal Ironworks, Kendal, in 1856 (see previous page). It was employed at Holmscales Farm near Kendal, and was of 5bhp, driving farm machinery for over a century before being offered to Messrs Gilbert Gilkes & Gordon.

The turbine wheel is placed on top for display only; water fell 30ft down the pipe near the front, and left through the centre. The 15in vortex Gilkes' turbine in the lower picture (1910) was used at Lowwood Gunpowder Mill to generate electricity. This is No 2145!

A turbine was different from a waterwheel in one important respect; it had a very high shaft speed, which had to be drastically geared down in order to drive mill machinery of the traditional kinds, but which could easily drive modern machinery. On the other hand, vortex turbines, which received water at the circumference, gained steadiness in operation from the centrifugal effect of the water, and were more steady in movement under variable loads. This picture, taken at Briery Mill near Keswick, shows details of hand controls, tree axles, crown and pinion gear and a section of line-shafting (upper part of picture by the light wall), the turbine, a Francis type of 75bhp, being in the pit below. It became common to install turbines in the pits formerly occupied by waterwheels.

Transport

After 1750 there were improved roads under turnpike trusts in this region. Some of their tollhouses can still be seen at roadsides, although the former are often of nineteenth-century date. The example shown below indicates the type of building to look for; this one is in Keswick, at the south-eastern entrance to the town, along the riverside.

Even after the advent of canals and railways, horse traffic continued to play a major part in Lakeland transport, wheeled transport for goods and passengers becoming much more important after the establishment of the turnpike trusts, that is, after about 1750. During the reign of Queen Victoria coach tours of Lakeland became well established, and many hundreds of horses provided this type of service for visitors. But these animals performed a variety of other functions, and besides working on numerous farm tasks of a familiar kind, they were put to turning gins like the device shown on the right which is now in Bowes

Museum. This has a more intimate relationship with road transport than might appear, and was a massive four-horse gin (later one-horse gin) used for crushing feed oats, and possibly for threshing barley for the local maltsters, kept as part of the equipment of a carrier's establishment at Dalton-in-Furness. Nearby were stalls for twenty-four horses, a harness room and lofts. There was a very flourishing malting trade in the near vicinity, Dalton being the centre for Low Furness in the early nineteenth century (see p32), and there were then malt kilns within a few paces of this establishment, which is now (summer 1970) awaiting demolition. The local iron mines, meanwhile, used vast amounts of animal horsepower and the ore carts creaked along the nearby roads in hundreds, carrying their loads to local landing or rail points. The Dalton family of Fisher, who owned this stable and its equipment, became important iron ore agents. The stable is well over a century old.

Carriers played a most useful part on Lakeland roads before and after the opening of the railways, and in some matters of trade they provided the only means of transport. They carried bulk goods, such as cotton and tobacco, from Whitehaven and Lancaster to the manufactories and mills in the eighteenth century; and woollen goods went in quantity from the Dovers' mill at Underskiddaw, c1830, to Whitehaven, Newcastle and Peterborough. Walter Berry, carrier at the port of Milnthorpe between 1838 and 1863, took strings of carts regularly from the port of Lancaster to Kirkby Lonsdale, Sedbergh and Brough, and also to Kendal and Ambleside. He carried paper from the Milnthorpe mills to the Kendal area, saltpetre and sulphur from Milnthorpe port to the gunpowder works at Larkrigg (or Old Sedgwick), as well as salt from Cheshire and blacklead from London warehouses. His business records, now preserved at the Westmorland Record Office, afford some interesting insights.

Water transport spread inland in a very limited fashion, and the towns of Carlisle and Ulverston were linked with the sea by short waterways, while the Lancaster Canal reached Kendal in 1819. The impact of this waterway was considerable, but was not as great as that of the local railways, which brought the tourists in their thousands after the 1850s.

This picture shows one of the original warehouses of the Port Carlisle Canal (1819-23), to the south of its former merchandise basin at Carlisle, and a few hundred yards west of the Caldewgate entrance to the city. The warehouse has a datestone marked 1821 and is a striking if modest piece of architecture in brick, still used as a bonded store. The canal was opened with the aims of importing cotton for the factories of the locality, and of bringing in building materials, especially slate, to the growing town. It gave Carlisle access to the sea at a point 11¼ miles away, then known as 'Fisher's Cross', and at this point Port Carlisle appeared. This terminus, too, should be visited; the stonework and dry bed of the canal basin are still visible, although it is hard to imagine that steamers for Whitehaven, Liverpool and Ireland departed from this place well over a century ago. At the city end, the remains (like this warehouse) are more satisfying, and the economic effect can be gauged by noting the siting of, for example, Carr's biscuit works a short distance away. Despite the fact that six locks hindered movement along the canal, it was used for passenger transport until the opening of the railways destroyed it as a working concern. The great cotton firms kept freight charges very low for their own convenience, and the canal was never profitable. By 1854 a railway track was running along much of the canal bed.

The industrial development of Cumberland and Lakeland Lancashire owes very much to the nearness of sea transport. The development of Whitehaven commenced in or about the south-east corner of the present harbour, as shown in the above photograph. The earliest intensive mining took place along the hill behind the camera, and the coal was brought to seagoing vessels near the mouth of the Pow Beck, which entered the sea near the small fairground in the centre of the picture. The first part of the harbour to be partially enclosed by quays was in fact the area in front of the camera, although the earliest quay to be built was the Old Quay (1634-87), with its famous watchtower or lighthouse, which lies to the seaward outside the picture, but which is approached along the quayside at our feet. The Sugar Quay, immediately in front of the camera, was completed in 1735.

This was only the beginning of the construction of several vast enclosed areas—the sweeping outer quays are, for the most part, of nineteenth-century construction—and the visitor may well wonder how so small a town is connected with so great a harbour. The answer lies in the flourishing coal trade with Ireland from the seventeenth to the nineteenth centuries; from this remote corner of England came virtually the whole of Ireland's coal supply.

In the centre of the picture on page 97, just to the left of the small fairground, can be seen a sloping ramp with rails. This is a former slipway, and immediately beyond it is a 'patent slip' (of which some of the masonry only remains) which caught the attention of Sir George Head as he was writing his *Home Tour of the Manufacturing Districts* (1835). It was, as he explained, a mechanical combination of 'the windlass, the inclined plane, and the railway'. Ships were drawn out of the water 'upon a frame consisting of enormous longitudinal and transverse beams, and which frame moves upon castors . . . the [vessel] is floated above it, and as the tide ebbs, allowed to rest thereupon'. The vessel to be repaired was then dragged up two pairs of rails, an inner and an outer, along an inclined plane of 180ft, by means of a vertically operated double-handled windlass working through eight wheels and pinions by the efforts of fifty men. Five hundred tons could be lifted in this way.

This picture shows a stone mounting near the head of the slipway described, which has been thought by students to have provided a base for part of the gearing. But the matter was much complicated when old Whitehaven citizens asserted that the supposed windlass mounting was no such thing, but was the base of a single-track railway swing bridge which carried the line across the front of the shipyard at this point! We were therefore obliged to suspend judgement, and wisely, for an old air photograph showed the local citizens to be right.

The buildings shown in the pictures below will be thoroughly familiar to visitors and residents in Ulverston; the large building overlooks the turning of the main road to Barrow, and stands north of the present Ulverston station. It is in fact the first permanent Ulverston railway station, built before the construction of the line round Morecambe Bay to Carnforth, which was completed in 1857. The date of the print reproduced in the upper picture is uncertain, but it was probably made about 1855, soon after the Barrow-Ulverston line was completed. One of the Furness Railway's original 'Bury' 0-4-0 locomotives can be seen emerging from the station shed on the left. When the Carnforth (Ulverston and Lancaster) line was completed in 1857, the line continued past the site of the present station towards the south, and it is probable that the High Level station here shown was then turned to its more recent employment as a Goods Shed. The fine modern Ulverston station was completed in 1873. The earlier station is a much more capacious and ambitious building than was the FR's contemporary station at Barrow, the other terminal point of the then Furness line. Not surprisingly, perhaps, because Barrow was then a mere shipping point and agricultural village, and Ulverston was still the market centre and 'capital' of this part of Lakeland.

The spread of railways in Lakeland brought advantages to many a remote locality; the Cockermouth, Keswick & Penrith line, opened 4 November 1864 for goods, soon afterwards provided this halt for workers at the Briery Bobbin Mill, north-east of Keswick. The same company played an important part in providing excursions for northerners visiting Lakeland in the 1870s, and the rise of popular tourism resulted in the opening of the Furness Railway branch line to Lakeside, Windermere (1869). Even then, the majority of visitors to Lakeland were middle-class, and little real provision was made for the masses until the end of Victoria's reign, except at weekends and bank holidays.

The archaeology of railways is a rich subject; one can find 87-year-old FR rail chairs in a siding, and an even older FR monogram at Ulverston station. There are many other examples scattered throughout Lakeland—mid-Victorian platform seats with a squirrel motif at Grange-over-Sands, lamps and lamp brackets at several stations, booking offices, signal posts, railway housing, all belonging to another age. Further examples and illustrations will be found in Mr David Joy's interesting books, *Main Line Over Shap* (1967), and *Cumbrian Coast Railways* (1968).

The history of Lakes water transport is another large subject. One of its most striking relics is the recently restored steam gondola, built at Coniston Hall in 1859 for the Furness Railway, and in service, with one interruption, until 1940. Lake Windermere has not only seen motorboat trials, like Coniston Water, but the earliest waterborne aircraft. *Waterbird* (1911) was advertised by its inventors, the Lakes Flying Co of Windermere, as the first hydro-monoplane to fly in Britain; this picture shows a biplane model, and was taken near Cockshott Point, Windermere.

Town Growth and Trade

Several of the towns of Cumbria were largely created by specialised trades and industries within a comparatively short space of time; Whitehaven, Maryport and Barrow-in-Furness which are well-known places, or Millom and Cleator Moor which owe their existence to iron-mining, or Windermere and Seascale which were created by the operation and traffic of railway companies. The industrial archaeologist cannot be satisfied with the collection of what some critics see as mere ironmongery or squalid ruins; he must also be a student of ways of life and of the consequences of industry. The most remarkable result of industrialism was the moulding of the majority of people into town dwellers. This process can be studied with especial advantage in the largely rural Lake Counties, which supplied many migrants to the towns.

The view of Maryport (below) taken from the North Quay, shows the first part of the town to be developed, when it was brought to birth by Humphrey Senhouse in 1748-9. The earliest houses were on Shipping Brow, the opening to which can be seen in the centre of the distant quay. Afterwards the town grew up along the ridge on the horizon. Maryport was essentially a point for the exportation of coal, which was brought from the Senhouse coalmines at Broughton Moor 2 miles away, and loaded on to vessels on the far side of the river mouth shown in this picture. The trade of the town grew considerably in the century after its creation, and a variety of sea-based trades, including shipbuilding, appeared. The harbour is in effect the closed estuary of the river Ellen, although there are extensive nineteenth-century docks to the right of the river. Maryport, a more fascinating town than it has been possible to suggest here, is well worth a visit.

It is untrue that the growth of industry inevitably resulted in wholesale squalor. Whitehaven is a graciously planned town which, like many others, suffered from the ruthlessly rapid development and population growth of the nineteenth century Fortunately, many of its more gracious aspects are still worthy of preservation. Its architectural styles range from the strictly functional warehouse (above) to the ornate (left). The wealth accumulated through grimy, dangerous labour and speculation in slave-produced commodities, resulted in the most elegant showpieces in Cumbria; and coal nourished the architecture of Carlisle Spedding's town house, the doorway of which is shown here.

One of the salient weaknesses of architectural history as conventionally written, is that it ignores the dwellings of humble people. These solidly built workers' houses (below) at Backbarrow, Furness (c1800) represent, in externals, a form of model housing of their day. Unfortunately for those who would whitewash the past, they were back-to-back houses, and at one period were overcrowded to the extent of having roughly a family for each room.

The mid-Victorian iron ore miners' row at Bigrigg, near Egremont, Cumberland (above), comfortably occupied by television viewers a century later, is, despite its utilitarian style, in the West Cumbrian architectural tradition, with heavy window surrounds. The barrack-like Old Barrow Flats, built for Barrow shipyard workers in the 1880s, were erected under the dual influence of Clydebank housing tradition and of the philanthropist George Peabody, promoter of 'model' buildings for the working classes.

Just as Gorbals tenement-builders could apparently influence local architecture, so could railway companies. The Furness Railway Company, personified in its formidable general manager, Sir James Ramsden, encouraged a form of brightly patterned brickwork which was locally known as 'the railway style', and which appears here (above) at Haverthwaite station (c1872). The small building with single chimney by the roadside was the watch-keeper's hut for the point at which the rail vans from the Lowwood Gunpowder Mill crossed the road into Haverthwaite Station yard.

Local trade often engraves its history on shop-fronts, and so does the story of a social movement like consumers' co-operation. In both town and village, societies sprang up in the 1850s and 1860s. In the Lake District they were sometimes encouraged by liberal-minded gentry or yeomen, as at Hawkshead. The iron miners of Cleator Moor created a very flourishing society (1858), and this shopfront, with its fine ironwork (1876), fittingly commemorates this.

Unusual trade signs, too, are worthy of preservation. This wooden hog, to be seen in Stricklandgate, Kendal, advertises the now almost defunct brush industry of that town, which has operated for about a century and a half. The bristles on the animal are of Brazilian bass, and it is known to be roughly 100 years old. Messrs Gawith, Hoggarth's trade sign in Lowther Street, Kendal advertising a famous snuff industry, was almost certainly older, and the firm's blending house, also shown, is believed to contain the oldest snuff machinery in Britain. The original sign is to be replaced (1970).

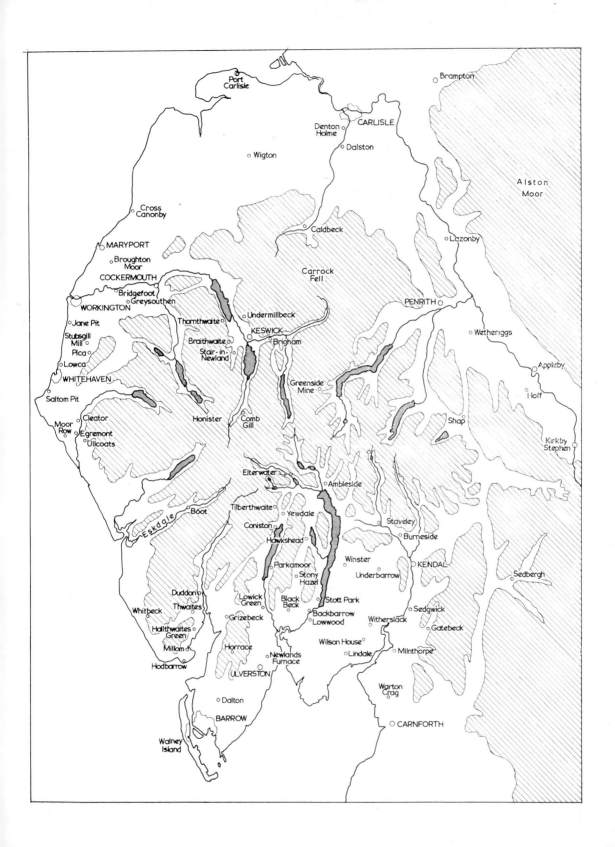

Sources and Acknowledgements

We should like to express our gratitude to the following for photographic assistance or permission to reproduce illustrations, and both where appropriate. Mr P. D. Scurrell, now of Barnard Castle, who gave splendid technical assistance throughout, and processed 128 of the photographs, took the upper photographs on pp 89 and 101, those in the lower page position on pp 23, 30, 47, 49, 83 and 86, and those in the sole position on pp 48, 70, 84, 88, 90, 95 and 99.

Kendal and Westmorland Public Library provided the pictures on p 17, the lower portion of p 42, and p 43, Ian Dalrymple of Kendal performing the processing; Mr Sam Hanna, ARPS of Burnley, kindly provided us with the picture of the clogger on p 45; Mr H. E. Evans kindly gave us the negative of the picture of Greenside mine on p 60; Mr John Anstee, of the Museum of Lakeland Life and Industry, permitted us to copy the sale bill on p 62; Mr J. J. Martin of Workington lent us the old photograph of Jane pit on p 52 and the views of the mining token on p 55; Gilbert, Gilkes & Gordon gave us permission to reproduce the Thomson turbine on p 92.

Our thanks also go to the Ministry of Defence, and the Ministry of Housing and Local Government, for permission to reproduce the air photograph (Crown Copyright) on p 69; the Talyllyn Railway Preservation Society for the advertisement on p 88; Miss Bairns and Mrs Gardner of Thornthwaite for the old photograph of Thornthwaite Lead Mine on p 58.

The view of Newland furnace in 1896 on p 80 is from the North Lonsdale Magazine.

M. Davies-Shiel took all other photographs (also providing the frontispiece and cover pictures), with the exception of the following, taken by J. D. Marshall: those in the sole positions on pp 24, 94, 96, 98 and 105, the upper left page position on p 78 and the lower positions on pp 58, 71 and 107.

Mr John Pendlebury gave his usual valuable help in processing and advice; Mr Joe Macmillan lent us the treasure of a photograph from which was traced the drawing of old Saltom pit on p 50; Mr C. Barter lent us the upper picture on p 42.

Helpful information, or permission to photograph, or both, were given by Messrs Carrs of Carlisle (whose staff member Mr Waugh we thank for his patient assistance); Mr Askew of Matthew Brown & Co, Cleator Moor Brewery; Messrs Jennings Bros Ltd of Cockermouth; Messrs Croppers of Burneside; Mr D. A. While; Messrs Robert Todd & Sons; and Mr R. B. Davis, formerly of the Hodbarrow Mining Co.

We are also grateful to Mr Eric Holland, Mr George Jepson, Mr John Braithwaite, Mr Paul N. Wilson, Dr R. G. A. Bunce, Mr A. H. F. Brown, and members of our history class at Ulverston for the trouble they have taken to help us at different stages. Mr Bill Norris has been a tower of strength throughout. Mrs K. M. Buckley was an efficient typist.

We thank our colleagues at the County Record Offices at Carlisle and Kendal for their unfailing help and ever-useful advice. Dr Arthur Raistrick's advice is also much appreciated.

Bibliography

Although there is a detailed bibliography in the authors' *Industrial Archaeology of the Lake Counties* (1969), to which we refer interested readers, the following background books will be found useful:

Bouch C. M. L., and Jones G. P., *The Lake Counties, 1500-1830* (1961)
Fell, Alfred *The Early Iron Industry of Furness* (1908, reprinted in 1968)
Lefebure, Molly *Cumberland Heritage* (1969)
Postlethwaite, J. *Mines and Mining in the Lake District* (3rd edn, 1913)
Rollinson, W. *A History of Early Man in the Lake District* (1967)
Schubert, H. R. *A History of the British Iron and Steel Industry* (1951)
Shaw, W. T. *Mining in the Lake Counties* (1970)
Somervell, J. *Water-Power Mills of South Westmorland* (1930)

Index

(This index includes the more important place-names, proper names and items not shown in the contents table.)